How to ..
Make Living Vases, Scre[...]
for Contemporary Floral Designs

First Published in Britain 2016
Author: Gill McGregor
Designs by: Gill McGregor
Copyright © Gill McGregor 2016
Published by: Gill McGregor College Publishers
ISBN 978-0-9929332-3-4
Printed in the UK
Layout design: www.sosbusyweb.co.uk

Coming Soon

**My Little Black Book of the Elements
& Principles For Floral Design**

*for Contemporary & Traditional
Floral Design*

Gill McGregor

I believe leaf manipulation has revolutionised the art of Flower Arranging and goes hand in hand with Contemporary floral design.

So I thought why not design a range of living vases, screens and structures using fresh foliage which are in water or water retaining materials to display and enhance our contemporary floral designs?

Other Books available from my website www.gillmcgregor.com/books
- Booklet 1 '5 days in a Hotel Bedroom' - a 'How to make' booklet focusing on Autumn and Winter designs
- Booklet 2 'Winning Thruppence shaped my career' – a 'How to make' booklet focusing on Spring and Summer designs

- '50 Techniques Used in Contemporary Floral Designs'
  ISBN 978-0-9929332-0-3
- 'How to.. Contemporary Floral Design - Wire Manipulation'
  ISBN 978-0-9929332-1-0
- 'How to' - Festive Winter Floral Designs
  ISBN 978-0-9929332-2-7

I have spent a year designing and developing a host of vases, screens and structures, some of which I have all ready taught during my workshops, for you to use.
As the majority of the foliage selected is evergreen, the vases, screens and structures very often out live the flowers.

This book instructs you with both written narrative and pictorial stages of development how to make each living vase, screen or structure for both floral designers and florists.

I have thoroughly enjoyed making this book as I specialise in how to use foliage in floral design to create distinction and hope you enjoy it too.

Living Ivy Screen

Cut a block of floral foam lengthwise to make 3 lengths measuring 2.5cms (1 inch) thick x 10cms (4 inches) x 23cms (9 inches). Secure with kebab sticks to make one long rectangular shape.

Cut a piece of OASIS® Copper Floral Mesh to measure 14 x 29 squares. Mould the mesh around the floral foam rectangle so that each side has a depth of one full square and the front and back are 6 squares wide; stitch to secure with wire.

To provide both extra support and a means of insertion, weave a 60cm (2 foot) wooden plant stick upwards through the mesh on one side leaving the last 10cms (4 inches) remaining to provide an insertion 'leg'. Repeat on the other side and then centrally at the back.

Lightly water the floral foam rectangle and place on newspaper to soak up excess water.

Select large Ivy (Hedera helix) leaves and base/cover the sides of the rectangle by arranging the leaves so that their stems are inserted in the front of the screen, allowing the leaves to curve around the sides neatly before pinning them into position at the back using 0.46mm green lacquered hair pin wires. Finish by basing (covering) the front and back with attractively positioned Ivy leaves inserted into the foam and strategically pinned so as not to be seen where necessary.

Select a suitable heavy container which is wider than the rectangle and fill with wet floral foam to 4cms (1½ inches) below the rim. Insert the rectangular structure towards the back and add an

additional piece of wet floral foam to the left front side, secure with a kebab stick.

Screw a lightly soaked 6 x 5cm OASIS® NAYLORBASE® LE BUMP®, 15cms (6 inches) down from the top right side of the screen.
Complete the design by arranging light weight flowers and foliage in the LE BUMP® and at the base of the design for effect.

Sculptured Rhapis palm, plaited Areca Palms, and mixed foliage have been arranged to enhance the Liatris, Carnations and Vanda Orchids for effect.

Carefully manipulate the stalk so that it curves and insert centrally into the square of floral foam and push the stem to go though the leaf blade and into the floral foam below. You have now created a 'basket shaped' Aspidistra leaf container.

Select a shallow glass dish and cut soaked floral foam to sit in the dish to a depth of 2½cms (1 inch). Cut a further piece of soaked floral foam to measure 6cms (2½ inches) square. Lay one Aspidistra elatior leaf onto the foam in the dish and position the square of soaked foam so it is on top of the Aspidistra leaf at its widest point and secure with kebab sticks.

Arrange flowers and foliage for effect, ensuring there is space visible to highlight the curved stem.

Manipulated Callas have been arranged for effect.

Using 1 bunch of Steel Grass (Xanthorrhoea australis), take 7 blades and weave down the outer column of the copper floral mesh until you can insert the stems into the wet foam.

Place a soaked 18cm (7 inch) posy pad with a 'hard biscuit' base onto a suitable shallow dish.

Cut a piece of OASIS® Copper Floral Mesh to measure 7 x 14 squares and curve lengthwise around a cylindrical waste basket. Sit the mesh to one side of the posy pad 2½cms (1 inch) in from the outer edge.

Push the blades down until they hit the 'hard biscuit' base. Repeat until each column has alternate woven Steel Grass.

Secure a small piece of wet floral foam with kebab sticks to one side and arrange light weight materials for effect.

Cut the sides of a block of floral foam to form a tapered vase shape - the base to measure 6cms (2½ inches). Using half a block of floral foam cut in half to form a square base 5cms (2 inches) thick. Soak the foam and secure the two components together with kebab sticks. Place on a shallow dish to collect excess water.

Cover the back and sides of the tapered foam vase, each with an individual Aspidistra elatior leaf. Insert the stem into the base and mould the leaf to neatly disguise the foam and secure with pins.

Roll the tips of 3 different width Aspidistra leaves and secure either side of the midrib vein with 0.46mm green lacquered hair pin wires. Take the widest rolled leaf, its roll level with the top, and measure the length required for the leaf to cover the front of the vase. Cut into the flesh of the leaf to achieve the length required, the midrib vein becomes the 'stem' and insert into the vase base. Pin the leaf to the foam, within the roll, for extra security. Repeat by adding the medium and then the narrower width rolled Aspidistra to create 3 neat rolls down the front of the vase.

Secure a small amount of wet floral foam with kebab sticks to the top of the Aspidistra Vase and arrange for effect.

I have used sculptured Rhapis excelsa and a woven Phormium tenax to aid distinction.

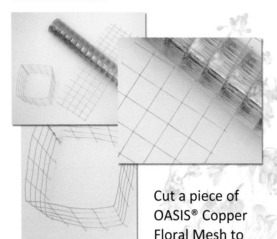

Cut a piece of OASIS® Copper Floral Mesh to measure 5 x 17 squares and remove the outer wire of the bottom 17 squares to form 'insertion legs'. Cut the outer wire away from one side to create wire prongs. Bend the copper mesh to make a 4 x 4 sided structure and secure together using the prongs.

Cut a piece of floral foam to be 2½cms (1 inch) larger than the mesh structure all the way round to a depth of 5cms (3 inches), soak and insert the structure centrally into the foam.

Wash 2 bunches of Bear Grass (Xerophyllum tenax) to remove any mud. Select circa 7

blades and place together so they are all flowing the same way. Insert the stems to weave down a column of wire mesh so that the grass flows outwards. Ease the stems into the foam. Repeat until all 16 columns have alternate woven Bear Grass.

Add an additional piece of wet floral foam into the square and secure with kebab sticks. Disguise the base floral foam and wire mesh with mixed foliage.

Complete the design by arranging flowers inserted into the central floral foam.

This design has wonderful physical movement.

Bear Grass Meadow Vase

P13

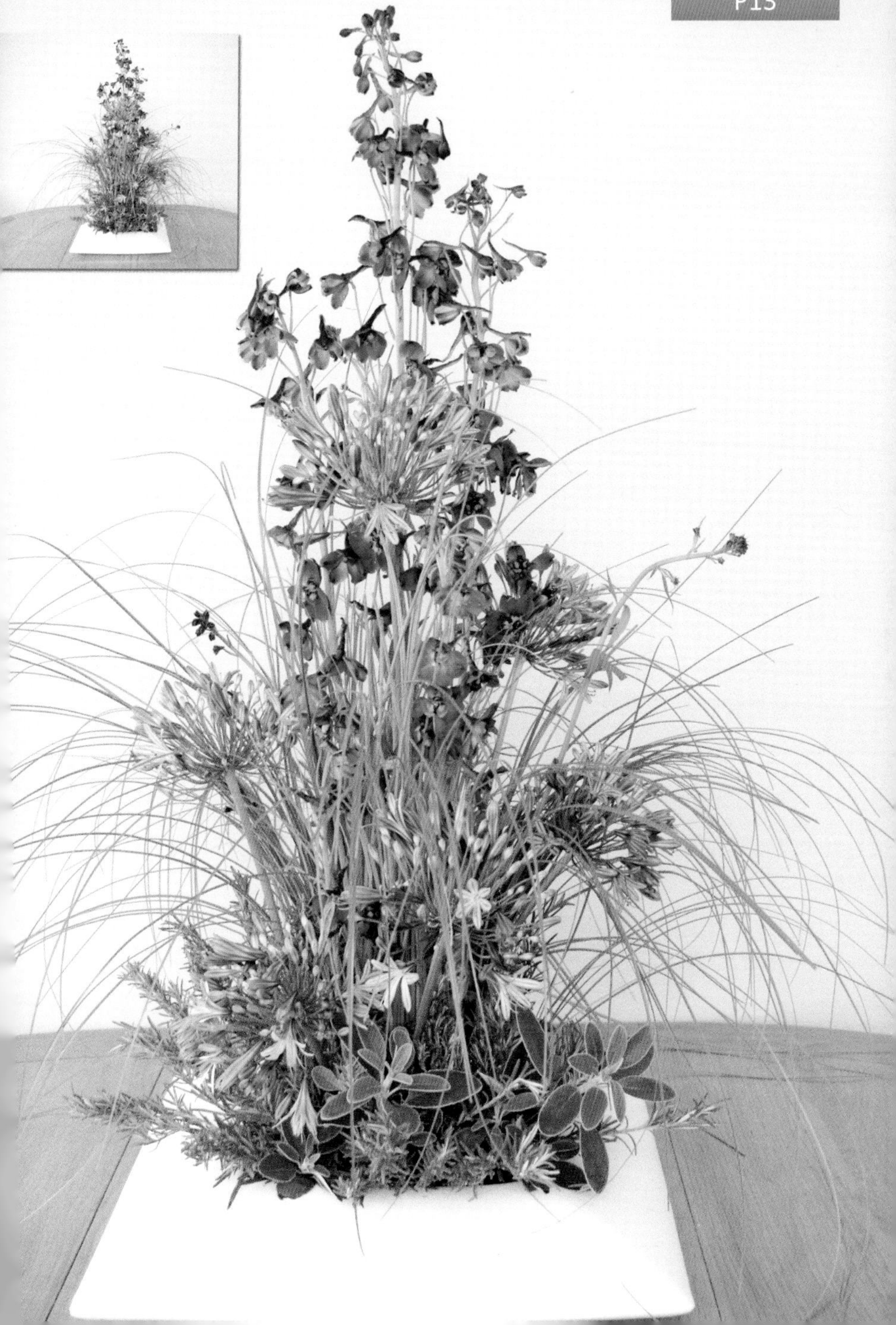

Using 18 Dracaena 'Green tie' leaves and half a block of wet floral foam in a plastic dish, decide upon the diameter of the design you require and take one Dracaena leaf and cut into the flesh either side of the midrib vein to the required length before ripping the flesh downwards to expose the main vein before cutting it to become a 'stem'.

Insert the cut down leaf at a diagonal angle into the side of the floral foam at the back so the leaf hides the floral foam. Take 2 identical width leaves and cut down to be slightly shorter and insert each one either side of the back leaf so their leaf edges buff up to the back leaf's midrib vein. Continue to cut down the Dracaena leaves in pairs, so they form a graded rosette shape which is up at the back and down at the front.

Arrange a further concentric ring of 8 cut down Dracaena leaves to produce this rosette vase.

Arrange choice materials in the centre of the design which add impact and distinction.

Cornus and Steel Grass Transparent Structure

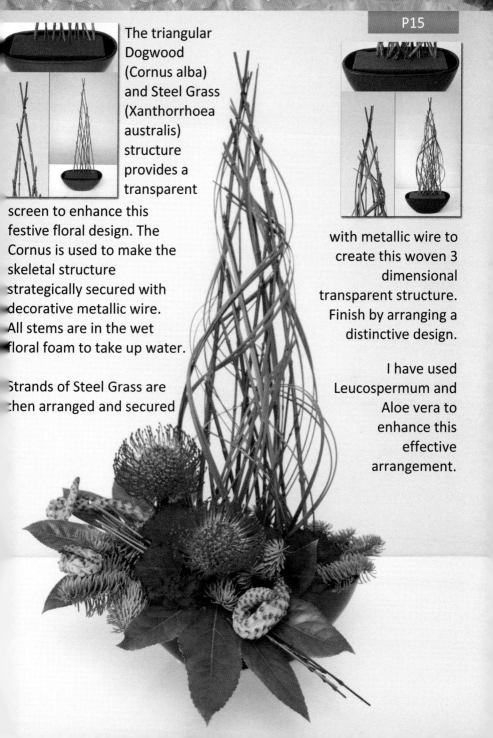

The triangular Dogwood (Cornus alba) and Steel Grass (Xanthorrhoea australis) structure provides a transparent screen to enhance this festive floral design. The Cornus is used to make the skeletal structure strategically secured with decorative metallic wire. All stems are in the wet floral foam to take up water.

Strands of Steel Grass are then arranged and secured with metallic wire to create this woven 3 dimensional transparent structure. Finish by arranging a distinctive design.

I have used Leucospermum and Aloe vera to enhance this effective arrangement.

Flowers that need lots of water are best arranged in a vase.

Select a glass rectangular or square vase which has a thin rim. Using 4 x 5cm (2 inch) Dogwood (Cornus alba) or equivalent stems, centrally split each stem half way up and push each split stem to straddle the vase's rim near each of the corners.

Cut a piece of OASIS® Copper Floral Mesh to cover the aperture of the vase with an additional square of mesh to bend round 2 sides. Position the floral mesh to be held by the corner sticks, above the rim, and secure with paper covered wire.

The mesh acts as the mechanic to support your arranged flowers and foliage. The Pussy Willow (Salix fragilis) is arranged in the vase through the mesh and secured together when it crosses an adjacent stem with paper covered wire. This acts as an aerial support mechanic for the large stems of the Amaryllis.

Amaryllis Vase Stem

Upturned Amaryllis filled with water survive very well and can also act as a vase for other flowers and foliage. The right hand upturned Amaryllis stem is secured into position with paper covered wire, filled with water and a single Amaryllis flower and Bear Grass (Xerophyllum tenax) are arranged in the stem for effect.

Pandanus Stacked Woven Screen

Cut a block of floral foam lengthwise in half, further cut to make a circa 23cm (9 inch) square and secure together with kebab sticks. Repeat with a second block of floral foam. Cut 2 x OASIS® Copper Floral Mesh to measure 11 x 20 squares and bend to form a 9 x 9 square cage with a depth of one square. Place a pre-prepared square of floral foam in each cage, secure in place with wire and slightly wet the foam.

Using a packet of Pandan leaves (Pandanus amaryllifolius) from a Chinese supermarket, base/cover each square using the weaving technique by inserting the leaves into the back of a foam square through the mesh, weaving the leaves at the front and pinning the tips at the back to hold in place.

Once both squares have been based, attach the squares to an upturned pedestal top with cable ties so the squares are stacked via their corner points. Pin a square of black bin bag to the back of each square for neatness. Place the stacked screen structure on a shallow dish and hide the pedestal base with aggregate.

Pandanus Stacked Woven Screen

Arrange 2 strategic placements through the Pandanus and link together with Flexi grass (Ficinea fascicularis) for effect.

Phormium tenax cube

Alternatively a cube of floral foam with a 'well' scooped out with a spoon can be based/covered in woven Phormium tenax and positioned on to a spiked base. A potted Primula has been inserted into the 'well' for effect.

This attractive plaited structure can be used to house flowers in a contemporary arrangement or as a hand tied framework. Wash the Bear Grass (Xerophyllum tenax) to get rid of any mud and secure as a bunch with an elastic band.

Place the Bear Grass bunch between your knees to hold with the tips uppermost. From the

Plaited Bear Grass Cone

outside take 9 adjacent blades, divide into 3s and plait for 10cms (4 inches). Slightly turn the bunch (always clockwise or anticlockwise; depending upon your preference) and plait a further four times. After the fourth plait, take from the bunch of Bear Grass 3 adjacent Bear Grass blades from the outside and nearest to the plait and lay on top of the 'braid' you have just plaited and slightly turn to your preferred direction. Plait 4 more times and again after the fourth plait lay 3 more adjacent blades on top of the 'braid' you have just plaited and slightly turn.

Keep plaiting uniformly without pulling the plait downwards; remember to add 3 blades each time after the fourth plait, slightly turning each time, and you will find the plaited area becomes a

spiral. Continue plaiting until there is no more grass to add and you have run out of 'braids'. Manipulate the plaited braid into a circle and secure with decorative wire to the plaited structure. Cut off any wispy blade tips for neatness.

Insert the structure into floral foam if to be used as part of a floral design. If used as a hand tied framework, carefully remove the rubber band, insert the flowers and foliage for effect and secure with string or a cable tie. Disguise the securing medium for effect.

If the rubber band is removed the plaited structure can be used for effect to enhance a design.

in a straight line so they touch the wire and pin the stems, half way down, together at the sides with black headed pins for added security.
Cut the top of the Equisetum as desired.

Complete the design with materials to hide the floral foam at the base and thread silk flowers through the structure so that their stems can be inserted into the foam at the back of the design.

This simple screen uses one bunch of 20 stems of Snake Grass (Equisetum hyemale).

Place wet floral foam in your selected container and mark out a straight line with a piece of wire attached to two wire posts. Deeply insert the Equisetum stems

Pin a piece of black plastic to go around the bottom and sides of the foam.

Cut a length of willow roll from a pound shop to a length of 40cms (15¾ inches). Stitch two 40cm x 1.80mm wires along each length of the wire stitched roll with metallic wire. Hot glue if required for additional security.

Bend the twig structure to house the floral foam boat shape. Cut 16 x 9cm (3½ inch) willow sticks and stack and glue together to make a pedestal foot.

Take a block of floral foam and using a 25cm (10 inch) plate, mark out 2 arcs which are 4cms (circa 1½ inches) apart. Cut the foam to create a boat shape.

Glue the foot centrally to the twig structure, insert the soaked foam and complete the design as desired.

Using a 14 x 7cm OASIS® Ideal Floral Foam Cake Dummie sitting in a fruit bowl, insert equidistant apart 9 x Cornus sticks measuring 20cms (8 inches).

As the sticks rest on the bowl's rim it will make all the sticks be positioned at the same diagonal angle.

Wet the foam and place the structure on a shallow dish.

Take 10 x 1 metre lengths of Ivy trails (Hedera helix) and insert one at a time into the floral foam and weave from the foam to the Cornus tips, securing each end with paper covered wire to form a transparent collar.

Complete the design with groups and clusters of flowers, foliage and sundries to make a central domed design.

I love the air of mystery this stand provides by using 6 Equisetum hyemale (Snake Grass) to support an aerial arrangement.

Take a 20cm (8 inch) posy pad with a 'hard biscuit' base and mark a central circle onto the foam measuring 12cms (5 inches) in diameter. Insert 6 x 1.8mm x 50cm black stub wires equidistant apart to go through to the bottom of the 'hard biscuit'. Thread a 35.5cm (14 inch) Equisetum onto each stub wire making sure they go all the way through the floral foam and touch the 'hard biscuit' base. Spiral the wires above the Equisetum and bind securely with black metallic wire so they are central to the circle below. Do not cut the wire. Bend the wires at a 90 degree angle just above binding wire. Do not allow the wires to cross. Commence the wire weave method around the stub wires to hold them equidistant apart to strengthen the platform upon which an OASIS® green junior bowl is placed.

Bend the 1.8mm wires around the bowl equidistant apart and position and secure wet floral foam using 6mm pot tape.

Pour a pint of water over the posy
pad and place on a flat plate.

Arrange the base of the design first to
provide greater weight and stability.

Finally select and arrange the top
second placement with light weight
materials for effect.

Bear Grass Transparent Posy Ring

Cut one block of floral foam in half lengthways. Place side by side to make a square and draw and cut out a circle measuring 16cms (circa 6½ inches) in diameter. Secure together with kebab sticks. Mark a central circle 6cms (2½ inches) in diameter and then a further circle 11cms (4½ inches) in diameter, soak and place on a flat dish to catch excess water. Wash the bottom of one bunch of Bear Grass (Xerophyllum tenax) and cut off the woody part of the blades' base. Measure and cut from the grass stem bases to a length of 32cms (12½ inches) and place in a pile. Keep the Bear Grass tips.

Commence arranging the Bear Grass by inserting the stems where the 2 circles are marked to create a looped transparent posy circle.
With the remaining Bear Grass, arrange loops to frame the outside of the transparent posy ring.

Arrange flowers and the tips of the Bear Grass in the posy centre.

Disguise the space between the Bear Grass stems with moss and arrange Ivy leaves to hide the remaining floral foam for effect.

Clamped China Grass Structure

Select a shallow square or rectangular glass dish with a thin rim. Cut wet floral foam to fit allowing space for foliage to be positioned to disguise the sides of the foam before placing in the dish.

Using 4 x 15cm (6 inch) Dogwood (Cornus alba) or equivalent stems, centrally split each stem for 2½cms (1 inch) and clamp by pushing each split stem down onto one of the 4 corners of the container's rim. Bind a small amount of paper covered wire around each stem, just above the rim, to hold the clamp in place.

Cut a piece of OASIS® Copper Floral Mesh to the size of the dish and attach to the top of each extended Cornus stem with paper covered wire.

Insert individual stems of China Grass (Liriope muscari) into the floral foam through the copper mesh and weave the tips to create a woven pattern until you have used one bunch of China Grass. Arrange water loving flowers and foliages above and below the mesh for effect. Top up the dish with water daily.

Puffed Rhapis Palm Vase

Cut out the semicircle of foam and then cut in half lengthwise to form 2 x semicircular pieces of floral foam.

Using a second block of foam cut off a sixth of foam and cut in half lengthwise and remove a small corner from each small piece. Place the 2 small pieces side by side lengthwise in the middle of the base with the cut corners on the outer edge. Place a semicircle of foam either side allowing a small gap between the central foam and each semicircle. Secure the semicircles into position with kebab sticks, making sure the base has a very small lip either side on the outer edges and remove the loose central foam.

Using a block of floral foam cut off a third lengthwise to act as the vase's base. Mark out a semi circle on the remaining 2/3 block of foam using a 23cm (9 inch) plate as a template.

Puffed Rhapis Palm Vase

Arrange Common Laurel leaves (Prunus laurocerasus) to cover the front sides of both semicircles; insert each stem in the base lip, 'wrap' position to cover the foam and pin the leaf tips inside the mechanics using hair pin wires. Insert at a slight diagonal angle a Finger palm (Rhapis excelsa) centrally into the base either side and individually wrap each 'finger' around the semicircle to create a puffed shape before pinning inside with a 56mm green lacquered hairpin wire.

Insert and secure the small lengths of floral foam inside the vase's structure and secure with kebab sticks. Place on a flat dish and water the foam.

Arrange as desired with the flowers and foliages inserted in both the base lips and the floral foam inside the vase.

Select a shallow round bowl and fill with wet floral foam to the level of the rim. Mark a 12.5cm (5 inch) diameter circle in the centre of the foam and insert at a slight diagonal angle 8 x 45cms (18 inches) Dogwood (Cornus alba) stems equidistant apart to form a circle with a diameter of 20cms (8 inches) at the top.

Wash and grade one bunch of Bear Grass (Xerophyllum tenax) into 3 different length piles.

Using the shorter lengths first, select circa 6 blades and insert, as a group, into the foam where the circle is marked and weave around the Cornus 'skeleton' and secure at the grass tips with green paper covered wire. Repeat inserting groups of Bear Grass strategically around the marked circle. Weave and secure each group to make a visually even, transparent woven structure.

As the woven structure increases in height use the medium and then the longest Bear Grass to gradually form a transparent vase.

Use one bunch of Steel Grass (Xanthorrhoea australis) to weave groups of 3 blades around the top of the 3 dimensional vase screen and secure in place with green paper covered wire.

Finish by manipulating 4 Dogwood (Cornus alba) stems around the Transparent Vase for effect and secure in place with green paper covered wire.

Arrange your selected materials to be inside and outside the Transparent Vase Screen for effect. Disguise the remainder of the floral foam with moss.

P34

Place a tumbler glass just 1cm (circa ½ inch) away from the edge of a 20cm (8 inch) posy pad with a 'hard biscuit' base and push down.

Remove and cut away the soft floral foam, in one piece, with only the tumbler size piece of floral foam remaining.

Insert 2 sticks 15cms (6 inches) apart, as legs, into the 'hard biscuit' medium. Soak the round of floral foam before inserting the raised screen into a suitable container with wet floral foam.

Commence arranging concentric layers of foliage to hide the 'hard biscuit' foundation by inserting their stems into the wet round foam. Pin the leaf blades into position, when necessary, to keep perfect placement.

For effect, select very different forms/ colours of foliage. Finish with a tastefully arranged spray and base design.

Alternatively this design can be placed on a circular dish, without the 'legs' and used as a coffee table design.

The Finger palm (Rhapis excelsa) has been cut at the tips to echo the plate's outline shape for effect.

Create this design using the single piece of wet foam cut away from the 20cm (8 inch) posy pad (page 34); with a 'hard biscuit' base. Support the weak area of foam with the hole by binding a one square length of OASIS® Copper Floral Mesh, in strategic areas with 6mm pot tape.

The China Grass (Liriope muscari) is inserted in the back of the foam to base/cover, in close neat order, with each blade's tip pinned for security at the back. Finish with a small selection of flowers and foliage which are inserted in between the China Grass blades.

Fan Palm Clam

Cut a piece of floral foam so that it has a step either side, soak with water and place in a shallow dish. Using 2 Fan Palm leaves (Serenoa repens) insert to echo the look of a clam.

This Clam container frames a design of a focal pineapple with Gingers (Heliconia), plaited Areca palms and rolled Dracaena leaves for effect.

Select a flat dish and cut wet floral foam to size. Sort, well conditioned, Common Laurel leaves (Prunus laurocerasus) into different size piles. Using the larger leaves arrange at the base positioned at a slight diagonal angle so each side of a leaf at the widest point buffs up to the midrib vein of it's neighbouring leaf; to form a concentric layer. Repeat creating a frilled concentric layer of medium sized leaves; again arranged at a slight diagonal angle.

Repeat to form a third layer of small Laurel leaves.

Arrange short flowers and foliage for effect.

Red roses finish the design to provide a complementary colour harmony. Pine has been added for both recession and textural interest.

Leaf Spheres

Using a flat, oval shaped leaf, for example Brachyglottis greyi (also called Senecio greyi), base/cover the sphere in concentric rings, starting from the top. Insert the leaves into the top of the sphere so they curve around the well's edge before pinning to secure in position. Repeat until the entire sphere is covered, the bottom ring of leaves' stems to be inserted in the base of each sphere. Repeat by basing the second sphere.

Using two wet foam spheres measuring 16cms (6½ inches) and 9cms (3½ inches) cut a piece off the bottom of each to sit flat. Cut off the tops and using a glass, push down and through the top of each one to create a 'well' when placed back on each sphere and secure with kebab sticks. Lightly soak the foam so it is still easy to hold.

To complete the design, arrange selected materials and inter connect using Flexigrass (Ficinea fascicularis) for effect.

Cut down an empty 2 litre plastic drinks bottle to a height of 20cms (8 inches). Fill with floral foam. Place 2 rubber bands around the cut off bottle – both 3cms (1 inch) in from the top and bottom.

Internally support wire, from the bottom and top, 2 bunches (40 stems) of Equisetum hyemale (Snake Grass) with 0.90mm x 35cm Green Lacquered Stub Wires.

Insert the Equisetum between the bottle and the rubber bands in close order until it disguises the outside of the plastic bottle. Cut the Equisetum top and bottom so both are level. Cut into the Equisetum at the top to create a 'V' shape at the front for effect. Pin the tips together, if required, with black steel pins.

Place the Cylindrical Equisetum Vase in a shallow dish of water. Soak the floral foam in the vase and add a small piece of wet floral foam in the dish to one side. Complete the design as required to produce a 2 placement arrangement.

Attach a 30cm (12 inch) OASIS® Styropor Half Ring and position on top of a soaked 36cm (14 inch) wreath ring and secure with stub wires.

Leaf manipulate 2 bunches x 10 Aspidistra elatior leaves to form individual rolled leaf tips.

Make the rolled leaves of different lengths by cutting into the leaf blade thus making the midrib vein the stem.
To base/ cover the foam and Styropor foundation insert a rolled leaf stem into the wet foam

Rolled Aspidistra Posy Ring

underneath the Styropor ring on the inside. Mould the leaves around the half ring neatly and pin to secure.

Repeat making sure the leaves slightly overlap to hide the foundation and that they are of different lengths to aid distinction.
Attach a small amount of floral foam to the top of the based

foundation with hair pin wires and arrange flowers and foliage for effect.

Place the completed design on a shallow dish to catch any excess water.

3 Dimensional Equisetum Trellis

Take one bunch (20 stems) of Equisetum hyemale (Snake grass) and insert a 1.1mm x 40cm green lacquered wire down each stem from the tip.

Using a 20cm (8 inch) posy pad with a 'hard biscuit' base insert 20 x 1.8mm x 50cm black stub wires randomly in the posy pad, making sure the wire goes through to the bottom of the 'hard biscuit' base for security.

Cover each aerial stub wire with a piece of Equisetum making sure the stem end is pushed into and down to the bottom of the floral foam. Bend as desired each Equisetum stem to form a 3 dimensional living trellis; the internal wiring will keep the bent Equisetum in position. Place the posy pad into a shallow dish which holds water; Equisetum is a water loving plant.

Select light weight materials to arrange as the floral foam is not deep. The living trellis will support weak stemmed flowers. Disguise the remaining floral foam with moss.

Fan Palm Looped Vase

Turn a block of floral foam on its end. Cut down the individual 'fingers' of the Fan Palm (Serenoa repens) into 10cm (4 inch) lengths. Insert each length to base/ cover the floral foam in decorative rows, creating your desired pattern. When covered, soak the foam and cut an additional piece of wet foam to sit on the top, secured with kebab sticks as the medium to arrange your materials in.

Place on a small dish.

This design includes cut-sculptured Areca palms, the cut base of the Fan Palm leaves, loosely knotted Flexigrass (Ficinea fascicularis) and Ornamental Kale (Brassica oleracea) for distinction.

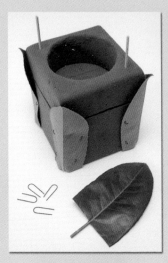

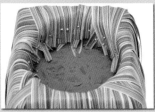

Cut one block of floral foam in half. Cut one of the halves in half again which when stacked will form a rectangular shape. Using the smaller piece of floral foam, insert a drinking glass into the centre of the foam to make a circular hole. Secure the 2 pieces of foam together with kebab sticks.

Cover each corner of the vase by inserting a Laurel leaf, underside showing, into the bottom of the vase. Wrap the leaf around each side of one corner and pin the tip to secure. Repeat to disguise each corner with a laurel leaf.

Using 2 bunches of China Grass (Liriope muscari), individually insert one blade of China Grass in the bottom of the floral foam, wrap around the side of the foam vase and curve the blade's tip to go down into the well and pin to secure with a steel dress making pin. Repeat to cover all 4 sides with China Grass in close, neat order.

Pour water into the well to soak the floral foam and place the China Grass vase onto a shallow dish to catch any water draining out.

Arrange your selected flowers and foliage for effect. This living vase can last circa 2 weeks if kept watered and placed in a cool position.

An alternative to the China Grass Rectangular Vase can be achieved by using a floral foam sphere; prepare as described on page 38 and base/cover in close order with Lily Grass (Liriope gigantea).

P46

Loose Woven Phormium Vase

Turn a block of floral foam on its end, take a second block of foam cut in half and cut in half again to make a square base plinth. Secure together with kebab sticks.

Base/cover the sides of the floral foam block by inserting Ivy stems (Hedera helix) in the front of the vase so the leaves wrap around the sides and pin the leaf tips at the back.

Finish by covering the front and the back with Ivy to cover the stems and the floral foam. Pin when necessary for extra security.

Take 7 pliable Phormium tenax leaves.

Use 3 for the front and 1 each side and insert the leaves in to the base plinth. Allow a small amount of space to be evident before inserting the tip into the top of the foam.

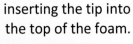

Weave 2 further Phormium tenax leaves horizontally as desired.
Insert each leaf into the back of the vase. Weave through the vertical Phormium and pin the tips at the back to hold in position.

Complete the design as desired.

Heliconia Living Vase

The Heliconia's (Lobster-claw) 'beak like' bracts house insignificant small flowers and the space within the bracts can contain a small amount of wet floral foam to arrange a small rose and complementary foliage for effect, thus providing a living vase when the stem is placed in water or water retaining material.

Cut a floral foam block lengthwise in half and secure together before marking out a circle measuring 15cm (6 inches) in diameter with a bowl and cut out the circle. Repeat with a

second block of floral foam and stack the 2 circles on top of a 20cm (8 inch) posy pad with a 'hard biscuit' base. Secure with kebab sticks.
Lightly soak and place on a flat dish.

Using one bunch of 10 Aspidistra elatior leaves, cut to size 1.1mm

Green Lacquered Stub Wires to be 2½cms (1 inch) from the tip to the base of the leaf and secure the wire on the underside of the leaf with black electrical tape to support the midrib vein. I find electrical tape holds better than pot tape, but it can be seen through the leaf in bright light.

Frilled Aspidistra Vase

Manipulate each leaf to echo a 'wave' before inserting each stem into the foam to create a frilled collar with overlapping leaf blades. To disguise the stacked foam, insert 2 Aspidistra leaves so they wrap around the stems and foam and pin to secure.

Complete the design as desired and cage with Steel Grass (Xanthorrhoea australis).

Herringbone Bear Grass

Select a dish and cut floral foam to the length and width required to a depth of 4cms (1½ inches). Cut an additional small piece of floral foam for a floral spray and secure on top where desired with kebab sticks. **Do not soak**.

Using a washed bunch of Bear Grass (Xerophyllum tenax), cut the thicker yet more pliable grass into to 11¼cms (4½ inches) lengths. Insert individually into the dry foam at a diagonal angle, the cut blades 4cms (1½ inches) apart, and in groups of 5 in close neat order.

of the herringbone pattern. Start the second row, by inserting the cut grass, in the opposite direction, so that the 5 x blades per 'bone' come from within the previous row's 'bones'. Repeat to cover with as many rows of herringbones as required. The secret is not to make a mistake so there are no holes evident in the floral foam. Finish the outer edges of the foam with level, neatly positioned and pinned Common Laurel leaves (Prunus laurocerasus) so the tips slightly curve into the design. Cut the bottom of the leaves level with the foam.

Leave a space measuring 1¼cms (½ inch) and repeat to create the first row

Soak the foam and place on a suitable flat dish with water.

Complete by arranging a spray of flowers for effect.

The herringbone pattern can be used as a means of basing in funeral work.

Herringbone Rhapis Palm 'fingers' have been used to create this herringbone pattern with Ming fern (Asparagus umbellatus) to hide the mechanics.

Make 9 Aspidistra Cones by manipulating an Aspidistra elatior leaf so that the tip of the leaf crosses over the base of the leaf to make a cone shape with a small hole at the base. Both the tip of the leaf and the stem will point upwards.

Fold the leaf tip into the cone so it follows the line of the leaf.

Turn the cone round so the stem is furthest away from you and carefully thread the stem down through the hole and staple to secure.

Position a Rose and a small amount of Lady's Mantle (Alchemilla mollis) in each cone as desired by threading their stems through the Aspidistra cone's hole and secure in position with paper covered wire.

Select the largest cone and place 2 large cones either side so they lock in position.

Place the remaining six around the first 3 cones, so again they lock in as a front facing design.

The stems are parallel.

Secure with string or a cable tie. Arrange looped Aspidistra leaves around the cone structure, stems parallel, position as desired and secure.

Alternatively,
each flower cones' stems
are cut down and placed in
a test tube of water and can
be inserted into the Urn or
Silver Vase Plant (Aechmea
fasciata) leaf base rosette
structure; to echo the look
of an Epergne.

Floating Square Screen

Make a square in the same way as the Pandanus Stacked woven screen on page 18.

Cut half a block of floral foam in half to form a square base and thread down a metal spiked stand. Prepare 7 x 17.5cm (7inch) lengths of Snake grass (Equisetum hyemale) and slide the first over the spike and arrange the remaining 6 around it to complete the disguise. Insert the floral foam mesh square onto the spike at one of the corners until it rests on the Equisetum. Lightly water the 'floating' square and base floral foam and place on a dish to catch excess water.

Screw a lightly soaked 6 x 5cm Oasis® Naylorbase® Le Bump® onto the top right side of the screen.

Arrange 6cm (2½ inch) lengths of Blue Pine around the sides in close, neat order. Base/cover the front with Blue Pine in close neat order and cut and secure a square of black plastic to cover the back for neatness.

Finish by arranging a spray of light weight flowers for effect in the LE BUMP® and base floral foam.

Take a 20cm (8 inch) posy pad with a 'hard biscuit' base and mark a central circle onto the foam measuring 12cms (5 inches) in diameter. Insert 6 x 1.8mm x 50cm black stub wires equidistant apart to go through to the base of the 'hard biscuit'.

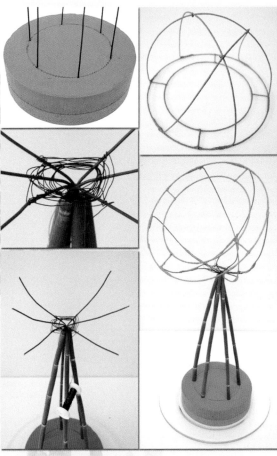

Thread each 35.5cm (14 inch) Equisetum onto each stub wire making sure they go through the floral foam and touch the hard biscuit base. Spiral the wires above the Equisetum and bind securely with black metallic wire so they are central to the circle below. Do not cut the wire. Bend the wires at a 90 degree angle just above binding wire. Do not allow the wires to cross. Commence the wire weave method around the stub wires to hold them equidistant apart to strengthen the platform and curve the stub wires upwards.

Take a 20cm (10 inch) flat copper wreath ring and 3 x 1.80mm x 50cm wires and tape with green florist tape. Curve the 3 wires around a cylindrical waste basket and bend each end of the wires 2½cms (1 inch) in at a 90 degree angle. Secure the wires to the outer wreath ring equidistant apart to create a partial sphere with the wires crossing to make a central triangle. Secure the partial sphere to the curved wires above the Equisetum legs, equidistant apart, with metallic wire and tape. Using a cut down OASIS® green junior bowl – add wet floral foam and secure with pot tape; so that it sits firmly on the wire weave platform.

Arrange the posy pad with low, grouped materials. **Important for adding weight at this stage for stability!**

Insert Ivy trails (Hedera helix) in the junior bowl's floral foam before weaving the Ivy through the partial sphere for effect. Secure the Ivy tips with paper covered wire. Finish by adding a few choice flowers to enhance the inside of the Ivy Sphere.

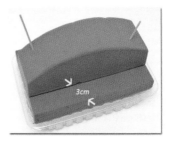

Mark out an arc on a block of floral foam using a plate as a template and cut out the curved foundation. Cut a further rectangle of floral foam 14cm x 23cm (2 sections) and place the curved foundation on to the rectangular base to provide a lip 3cms deep for each of the long sides and secure with kebab sticks.

Soak the foam and place on a flat tray to collect excess water.

Cut circa 48 x 15cm (6 inch) straight lengths of Equisetum, dependent upon their diameter; to provide sufficient cover. Start to insert Equisetum into the lip right up against the curved foundation to form a 'fence'.

Pin the Equisetum together to make sure no gaps are visible, using black headed pins. Cut the tops of the Equisetum to echo the arc of the curved foundation. Repeat with the other side.

Arrange and pin leathery leaves to hide each of the sides of the curved foundation.

Complete the design by arranging materials in each of the foam 'lips' to hide the tray placed on a complementary base before adding a decorative band of flowers and foliage as desired.

Cut out the semicircle of foam and then cut in half lengthwise to form 2 x semicircular pieces of floral foam.

Using a block of floral foam, cut off a third lengthwise and cut in half lengthwise again. Mark out a semicircle on the remaining 2/3 block of foam using a 23cm (9 inch) plate as a template.

Stack the 2 lengthwise slithers on top of each other and place a semicircle of foam either side. Secure with kebab sticks.

Cover the foam as before (see page 30) with the Common Laurel (Prunus laurocerasus) and then with the Rhapis palms (Rhapis excelsa); all the stems being inserted into the top stacked slither of floral foam.

Cut out a small round of wet foam with a round pastry cutter and secure centrally with kebab sticks. Place on a flat dish and add water.

Complete by arranging a small spray of flowers and foliage for effect.

Using a 14 x 7cm OASIS® Ideal Floral Foam Cake Dummie place on a shallow dish and cover the sides with flat Cupressus inserted at an acute diagonal angle with the tips pinned into position. Add loops of Bear Grass (Xerophyllum tenax) and China Grass (Liriope muscari) evenly around the sides to disguise the Cupressus.

Finish the top of the 'cake' with groups of flowers and foliage for effect with additional Bear Grass loops veiling the placements.